Success

Assessment Papers

English

8 – 9 years · levels 2 – 4

Alison Head

Sample page

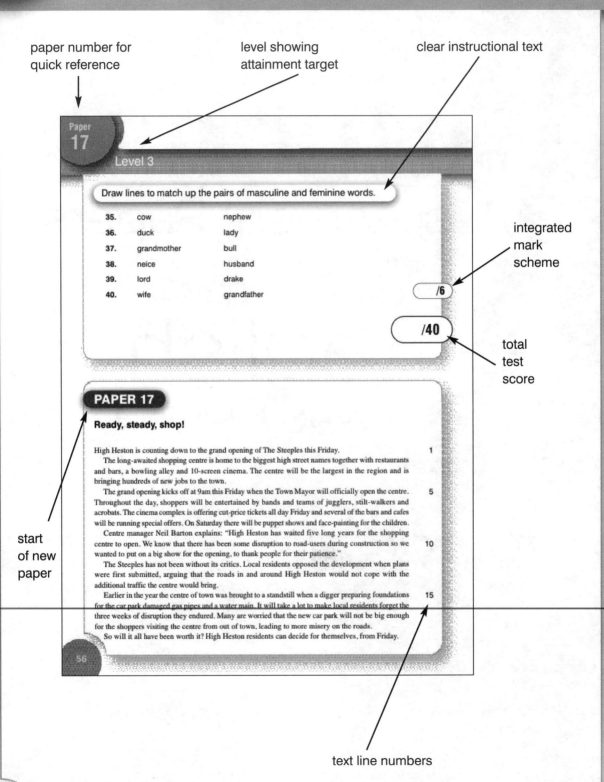

paper number for quick reference

level showing attainment target

clear instructional text

Paper 17

Level 3

Draw lines to match up the pairs of masculine and feminine words.

35.	cow	nephew
36.	duck	lady
37.	grandmother	bull
38.	neice	husband
39.	lord	drake
40.	wife	grandfather

/6

/40

integrated mark scheme

total test score

PAPER 17

Ready, steady, shop!

High Heston is counting down to the grand opening of The Steeples this Friday.   1

The long-awaited shopping centre is home to the biggest high street names together with restaurants and bars, a bowling alley and 10-screen cinema. The centre will be the largest in the region and is bringing hundreds of new jobs to the town.

The grand opening kicks off at 9am this Friday when the Town Mayor will officially open the centre.   5 Throughout the day, shoppers will be entertained by bands and teams of jugglers, stilt-walkers and acrobats. The cinema complex is offering cut-price tickets all day Friday and several of the bars and cafes will be running special offers. On Saturday there will be puppet shows and face-painting for the children.

Centre manager Neil Barton explains: "High Heston has waited five long years for the shopping centre to open. We know that there has been some disruption to road-users during construction so we   10 wanted to put on a big show for the opening, to thank people for their patience."

The Steeples has not been without its critics. Local residents opposed the development when plans were first submitted, arguing that the roads in and around High Heston would not cope with the additional traffic the centre would bring.

Earlier in the year the centre of town was brought to a standstill when a digger preparing foundations   15 for the car park damaged gas pipes and a water main. It will take a lot to make local residents forget the three weeks of disruption they endured. Many are worried that the new car park will not be big enough for the shoppers visiting the centre from out of town, leading to more misery on the roads.

So will it all have been worth it? High Heston residents can decide for themselves, from Friday.

56

start of new paper

text line numbers

2

Contents

PAPER 1

It had been a thoroughly ordinary Thursday. Assembly in the hall was followed by a maths test. Playtime was inside because of the rain, then PE and art, which was making firework pictures on black paper with coloured chalks. Cheese spread sandwiches for lunch, then more wet play. English came after lunch, writing stories about the autumn.

It was strange, then, that the walk home from school should turn out to be quite so extraordinary. As usual, Joe walked with his friend Max as far as the corner, before saying goodbye and heading for home in the next street.

"Excuse me," said a voice, politely. "I appear to be a bit stuck." Joe looked up and down the empty street. He thought he must be hearing things. After all, what would you think if you heard someone speaking to you when there was nobody there?

"Please don't walk past!" begged the voice. Listening carefully, Joe followed the sound of the voice across the pavement. It seemed to be coming from… Joe peered down the drain and found himself gazing into a pair of large, scared eyes. He gasped.

Circle the correct answers.

1. What was Joe's first lesson after assembly?

English   maths   art

2. What was in Joe's sandwiches?

jam   ham   cheese spread

3. What was Joe's friend called?

Martin   Mark   Max

Answer these questions.

4. How did Joe make his firework picture?

_____

_____

5. What was the weather like in the story?

_____

6–7. The story takes place in the autumn. Write down two things in the story that tell you that.

_____

_____

8. Explain in your own words how you would feel if you heard a voice speaking to you when there was nobody there.

_____

_____

_____

_____

9. What do you think the word *gasped* means in the final line of the text?

_____

_____

_____

10. Why do you think Joe gasped when he saw a pair of eyes looking at him from the drain?

_____

_____

/10

> Underline an **adjective** in each line.

11.	book	speak	green	buy
12.	happy	farm	give	school
13.	Sunday	beach	huge	ear
14.	dark	journey	friend	prettily
15.	tea	build	under	frosty
16.	shoe	dog	soft	box

/6

Write down a *le* word for each picture.

17. _____   18. _____

19. _____   20. _____

21. _____   22. _____

/6

Add the prefix *un* or *dis* to make antonyms.

23. _____happy   24. _____qualify   25. _____appear

26. _____fair   27. _____pack   28. _____agree

/6

Write down the separate words that make up these **compound words**.

29–30. doorbell   _____   _____

31–32. cheesecake   _____   _____

33–34. earring   _____   _____

/6

Write these words again, in **alphabetical order**.

green   orange   pink   blue   purple   red

35. _____   36. _____

37. _____   38. _____

39. _____   40. _____

/6

/40

PAPER 2

The Sahara Desert

The Sahara is the world's largest hot desert. It covers more than nine million square miles,   1
making it larger than Australia and almost as big as Europe.

The desert covers vast areas of North Africa including large parts of Egypt, Libya, Tunisia,
Chad and Morocco. It was once a much wetter place than it is today, and fossils show
that dinosaurs once lived there. Today, most of the Sahara is covered with rocks and   5
sand dunes, which can reach 180 metres high.

Two and a half million people live in the Sahara Desert, mostly in Egypt, Algeria, Tunisia
and Morocco. Out of the cities, people use dromedary camels to get about. They are
specially adapted for life in the desert, with large, flat feet for walking on the sand
and long eyelashes to keep sand grains out of their eyes. They use their fatty humps to   10
store water, enabling them to stay in the desert for long periods of time. Their thick coats
help to keep them warm when the temperatures drop sharply at night.

Few plants grow in the desert apart from in the fertile Nile valley and in oases, which are
lakes made by natural spring water. The Nile is the world's longest river and Egypt's people
have relied on its waters for survival for thousands of years. The ancient Egyptian   15
civilisation grew up along its banks and the remains of countless temples and pyramids
can still be seen today, preserved by the hot, dry desert air.

Circle the correct answers.

1. The Sahara Desert is almost as large as which continent?

Europe   Asia   America

2. Plants grow in oases in the desert. Why do you think this is?

because oases have water   because oases are dry   because oases have sand

Answer these questions.

3–5. List three countries covered by the Sahara Desert.

_____   _____   _____

6. How do we know that dinosaurs once lived there?

_____

_____

7. What does the word *dune* mean in line 6?

_____

_____

8–9. Write down two ways that camels are adapted for life in the desert.

_____

_____

10. Explain in your own words why an animal that lives in the desert might need a thick coat.

_____

_____

/10

Underline the **homonym** in each pair.

11.	saw gate		**12.**	room right
13.	learn tap		**14.**	ball flower
15.	train rug		**16.**	light pen

/6

Write down the **plural** form of these **singular nouns**.

17. egg _____

18. dish _____

19. glove _____

20. witch _____

21. bus _____

22. zoo _____

/6

Underline the **verb** in each sentence.

23. The girl climbed the stairs.

24. Flowers grow in the park.

25. A flock of birds flew over our garden.

26. My brother plays basketball for his school.

27. The cat balanced on the fence.

28. Sarah wandered slowly to school.

/6

Circle the words that have two **syllables**.

29–34.
hospital	pillow	rabbit	house
follow	beach	candle	computer
coach	fortune	bubble	

/6

Add the **suffix** *ful* or *ly* to each of these words.

35.	kind_____	36.	hope_____
37.	forget_____	38.	actual_____
39.	like_____	40.	pain_____

/6

/40

PAPER 3

New Home for Newtown School

Councillors have blown the whistle on a school's plans for expansion with the announcement this   1
week that Newtown School will close at the end of the school year.

Head teacher Robin Shaw approached the council last year looking for funding to extend the
school buildings, which are no longer large enough to accommodate the school's 240 pupils.
Reviewing the application, the council has decided that the upkeep of the site, constructed in 1950,   5
has become too costly. It has purchased a site across town where a new school is planned. The current
Newtown site will be sold for housing development.

The decision has angered parents, who worry about the long and difficult journey their children
will face to get to school each day. Sally Groves, mother of eight-year-old Emily says, "It will take
Emily more than half an hour to walk to school and she will have to cross three major roads to get   10
there. If parents have to drive to the school, we'll just be adding to the rush-hour traffic. The council
hasn't thought this through."

Town Councillor Jenny Green disagrees. "As a council we have to make decisions about the best
way to spend taxpayers' money. Newtown School was constructed after the war with reinforced
concrete, which is now crumbling. It would not be practical to extend the existing buildings. The new   15
school will have fantastic facilities and enjoy better transport links, with a frequent bus service and
new pedestrian crossings. There will also be traffic-calming measures in the local area, including
speed bumps, to slow the traffic down.

Selling off the Newtown site to Harris Homes would also provide the council with a significant
source of income, enabling us to improve services to local residents. It is a win-win situation."   20

Local residents have until the end of next week to oppose the plan.

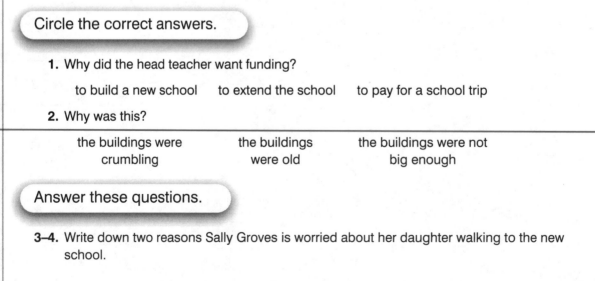

Circle the correct answers.

1. Why did the head teacher want funding?

   to build a new school   to extend the school   to pay for a school trip

2. Why was this?

   the buildings were   the buildings   the buildings were not
      crumbling   were old   big enough

Answer these questions.

3–4. Write down two reasons Sally Groves is worried about her daughter walking to the new
school.

_____

_____

5. Why does Jenny Green say that the existing school buildings could not be extended?

_____

_____

6–7. Explain in your own words two effects that the location of the new school might have on local roads.

_____

_____

_____

8. Give an example of a *traffic-calming measure* (line 17) that is mentioned in the text.

_____

9. Who wants to buy the old Newtown School site?

_____

10. What does Councillor Green mean when she describes the construction of the new school as a "win-win situation"?

_____

_____

/10

Add *there* or *their* to complete each sentence.

11. We will go sledging if _____ is snow.

12. _____ will be time to play after tea.

13. The boys left _____ muddy shoes by the door.

14. I love the park so we go _____ every Sunday.

15. The horses flick _____ tails to brush away the flies.

16. The actors learnt _____ lines for the school play.

/6

Write down an **antonym** for each word.

17. high _____   18. big _____

19. lost _____   20. empty _____

21. clean _____   22. tall _____   /6

Write these **present tense** sentences again, in the **past tense**.

23. Ben walks to school. _____

24. The girls collect shells on the beach. _____

25. I wish by the wishing well. _____

26. Mum bakes cherry cakes. _____

27. I switch on the lights at night time. _____

28. Sally brushes her long hair. _____   /6

Circle the correctly spelt word in each pair.

29. table   tabble   30. buble   bubble

31. carry   cary   32. happy   hapy

33. peper   pepper   34. summer   sumer   /6

Write down the words that have been joined in each **contraction**.

35. I'm _____   36. she'll _____

37. couldn't _____ 38. they're _____

39. he's _____   40. we'll _____   /6

/40

PAPER 4

Gingerbread men

Ginger is a natural flavouring made from the root of a plant. It is delicious in biscuits and cakes and is also used in Eastern cookery.

To make 16 gingerbread men you will need:

Ingredients
- 200g plain flour
- Pinch of salt
- 1 x 10ml spoon of ground ginger
- 75g butter or margarine
- 50g sugar
- 75g golden syrup
cutter
- 2 eggs
- Currants for decoration
- Flour for rolling out
- Butter for greasing the baking sheet

Equipment
- Weighing scales
- Mixing bowl
- Wooden spoon
- Rolling pin
- Baking sheet
- Gingerbread man

1. Heat the oven to 180° Celsius.
2. Thoroughly mix together the butter, sugar and syrup.
3. Add the flour, ginger and salt.
4. Beat the egg and add enough to the mixture to make a stiff dough.
5. Dust your work surface with flour to prevent the dough from sticking.
6. Use a rolling pin to roll out the dough half a centimetre thick.
7. Cut out gingerbread men with a cutter.
8. Add currants for eyes, noses, mouths and buttons.
9. Bake on a greased baking sheet for 20 minutes.
10. Allow to cool on a cooling rack before storing in an airtight container.

Circle the correct answers.

1. What kind of flour is used in the recipe?

self-raising   wholemeal   plain

2. What should you use to prevent the mixture from sticking to the work surface?

dust   flour   sugar

3. What are the currants for?

decoration   flavour   rolling out

Answer these questions.

4. What is a *natural flavouring*?

_____

_____

5. Explain in your own words what the phrase *pinch of salt* means.

_____

_____

6. Why do you think the syrup has the name *golden syrup*?

_____

_____

7. Why should you grease the baking sheet with butter?

_____

_____

Write down what these words in the recipe mean.

8. Ingredients _____

9. Equipment _____

10. Air-tight container _____ /10

Find the **proper nouns** then write them again with capital letters.

bag	swan	france	dog	october
monday	door	window	sally	liam
cushion	europe	lamp		

11. _____   **12.** _____   **13.** _____

14. _____   **15.** _____   **16.** _____   /6

Choose *am*, *is* or *are* to complete each sentence.

17. I _____ going to Spain on holiday.

18. My dog _____ called Wendy.

19. I can join the judo club when I _____ nine.

20. I like my cousins because they _____ great fun.

21. Owls _____ nocturnal animals.

22. It _____ cold today.

/6

Underline the **personal pronoun** in each sentence.

23. We were late because the alarm clock was broken.

24. Dad was delighted because he won the football match.

25. Mum made us pizza for tea.

26. I would love to go rock climbing.

27. You must cross the road carefully.

28. Mum and Dad are grumpy when they wake up in the morning.

/6

Circle a **synonym** for each of these words.

29. old	broken	ancient	short
30. ocean	sea	lake	watch
31. worried	cheerful	concerned	delighted
32. road	church	school	street
33. answer	question	reply	suggest
34. house	shed	home	sock

/6

Underline the **root word** inside each longer word.

35. export　　　　**36.** hopeful　　　　**37.** heroic

38. winner　　　　**39.** golden　　　　**40.** realistic

/6

/40

PAPER 5

Weird is the woman who lives in the woods　　　　1
and weird are the clothes she wears.
Crooked the roof of her gingerbread house
and crooked the rickety stairs.
Tattered and patched are the curtains that hide　　　5
the tattered and patched things decaying inside.

Sneaky and cheeky the children who spy,
leaving their safe little homes nearby.
Creaky and squeaky footsteps on the floor,
creaky and squeaky the hinge on the door.　　　10
No time to run from what stands there…
a tiny old lady with bugs in her hair.

"Come in my dears, I'm about to have dinner.
I'll disappear if I get any thinner!
I look forward to children coming to snoop,　　　15
it gives me something to put in my soup!"

Circle the phrase to correct this question.

1. What kind of stories do gingerbread houses sometimes appear in? Circle your answer.

　　crime stories　　　fairytales　　　science fiction stories

Answer these questions.

2–3. Write down two words that describe the stairs.

_____   _____

4. What does the word *decaying* mean in line 6?

_____

5. Why do you think the children come to spy?

_____

6–7. Write down two words in the second verse that describe sounds coming from inside the house.

_____   _____

8. What is unusual about the old lady's hair?

_____

9. What does the lady say she was about to do?

_____

10. What does she want to put in her soup?

_____   /10

11–16. Write these words again in **alphabetical order**.

come   grape   soil   camel   sausage   giant

1 _____   2 _____   3 _____

4 _____   5 _____   6 _____   /6

Pick a sequencing word from the box to fill each gap.

After, then, Next, First, before, finally

17–22. _____, Grandad filled little pots with compost, _____ using a pencil to make a little hole in the soil. _____, he dropped a seed into each hole, _____ he gently covered the seed with compost. _____ that he watered each pot carefully and _____ he placed them on the windowsill in the sunlight.

/6

Add the **suffix** *ship* or *hood* to these words.

23. child_____

24. knight_____

25. friend_____

26. boy_____

27. owner_____

28. neighbour_____

29. partner_____

30. member_____

/8

In each sentence, underline the words that someone has said.

31. "What a beautiful picture!" said the teacher.

32. Dad called up the stairs, "Have you seen my keys?"

33. Poppy shouted, "Great goal!"

34. "We'll be late if we don't hurry!" warned Mum.

/4

Add the **possessive apostrophe** in the correct place.

35. the dogs paw

36. the womans car

37. a cats tail

38. the girls foot

39. a towns roads

40. the boys nose

/6

/40

PAPER 6

The Heart of the Monkey
(based on an African Swahili folk tale)

A long time ago, a little town stood at the foot of a cliff. On the edge   1
of the town grew an enormous kuyu tree. It was so large that half of
its branches grew over the town and the other half grew out over the sea.

The branches of the tree were heavy with fruit and a large grey monkey sat in the tree
each morning to eat his breakfast. One day he noticed a shark watching him greedily.   5

"Oh, if only I could have some of that fruit. I am so tired of salty fish," complained
the shark.

The monkey threw down some kuyu fruit and from that day the monkey and the shark ate
breakfast together each morning. One day, the monkey said, "How I wish I could see all
the wonderful things in the sea."   10

The crafty shark replied, "Hop on my back and I will show you those things. I promise that
you won't even get wet."

The monkey agreed, and the pair set off together on a long journey. Six days later the shark
said, "I have something to tell you, monkey. Before we left on our journey, I heard that
the sultan of my country is terribly ill and can only be cured with the heart of a monkey."   15

The frightened monkey thought carefully, then replied. "What a pity you did not tell me
when I was still on land. Then I would have brought my heart with me."

"Whatever do you mean?" asked the puzzled shark.

"Surely you must know that when we go on a journey we leave our hearts hanging in a
tree, so that they will not trouble us?"   20

The disappointed shark said, "There is no point going on if you
don't have your heart. We had better go back for it."

The monkey was delighted, but careful not to show it. The shark swam quickly and within
three days they were back at the kuyu tree. The monkey swung himself into the tree. As
he disappeared into the branches he called, "Have a pleasant journey home. I hope you   25
find your sultan better!"

1. What sat in the tree to eat its breakfast? Circle your answer.

   a parrot   a monkey   a squirrel

2. Find and write down one word in the first paragraph that comes from another language.

   _____

3. What reason does the shark give for wanting some fruit?

_____

4–5. Find and write down two words used to describe the shark in the story.

_____   _____

6. What does the word *sultan* (line 15) mean?

_____

_____

7. Why is the monkey afraid in line 16?

_____

_____

8. Explain in your own words how the monkey tricks the shark into taking him back home.

_____

_____

9. How long, altogether, were the monkey and the shark travelling?

_____

10. Write a sentence to explain which of the animals in the story you think is wiser. Include evidence from the story.

_____

_____

/10

Add a **comma** to each sentence to mark where the reader should pause.

11. Anna wrote as neatly as she could not smudging the ink at all.

12. Tail wagging wildly the puppy chased the ball.

13. Not finding any boots she liked Nina bought some shoes instead.

14. When nobody answered the phone Max left a message.

/4

Add *ly* to these words to turn them into **adverbs**.
Remember to alter the spelling if necessary.

15. kind _____

16. pretty_____

17. actual _____

18. dainty_____

19. full _____

20. dizzy_____

21. rude _____

22. graceful_____

/8

Read this passage, then answer the questions.

The children of Jubilee Road all play together. Eight year-old Paulo lives at number 2, next to Laura who is nearly 10 and her older brother Mark, who is 12. Three doors down live twins Daniel and Christopher, who are nine. When it snows they all go sledging together and in the summer holidays they like to camp out in their back gardens. Whatever they do, Mark is normally in charge.

23. Who is the oldest child in Jubilee Road?

_____

24. How many of the children are nine years old?

_____

25. Who has no brothers or sisters?

_____

26. Suggest a reason why Mark normally takes charge of the group.

_____

/4

Circle the correct **diminutive** for each bold word.

27. pig	pigling	piglet	**28. duck**	ducklet	duckling
29. goose	gosling	gooselet	**30. cat**	catkin	kitten
31. swan	signet	swanlet	**32. horse**	calf	foal
33. bear	cub	pup	**34. kangaroo**	roo	joey

/8

Use one of the **conjunctions** from the box to complete each sentence.

when   because   before   but   so   while

35. We waited at our friend's house _____ Mum was finishing her work.

36. It was very funny _____ Dad fell over on the ice.

37. My sister won the prize _____ her entry was the best.

38. We bought the best tickets for the show _____ we would have the best view.

39. We ran to catch the bus _____ we were too late.

40. Dad made us breakfast _____ he left for work.

/6

/40

PAPER 7

Swanage, Dorset
A visitor's guide

The seaside town of Swanage lies at the end of the Purbeck peninsula. Its wide   1
sandy bay offers wonderful views of the Isle of Wight in fine weather, together with
the Old Harry Rocks, which stand in the sea at the North End of the beach.

As well as safe swimming, the bay also supports a variety of watersports, including
windsurfing and sailing. Holidaymakers can hire pedalos and motor boats to get   5
out on the water, or take part in organised fishing expeditions. Regular boat trips
also give visitors the chance to see the area's Jurassic coastline, which has been
named England's first World Heritage Site because of its geology.

Boats also visit nearby Poole, Bournemouth and Brownsea Island, which is home
to rare red squirrels. The beach also boasts one of Britain's oldest surviving Punch   10
and Judy shows.

The town itself has plenty to interest tourists. A restored steam railway takes visitors inland to Corfe, with its famous castle. The castle was destroyed during the English Civil War but remains as one of Britain's most striking ruins and is believed to be the inspiration for Kirrin Castle in Enid Blyton's *Famous Five* story *Five on a Treasure Island*.   15

Visitors to Swanage can take part in a variety of sports including golf, tennis, bowls and swimming. There are also miles of stunning cliff top paths nearby for keen walkers or the less energetic can stroll along the town's restored Victorian pier.

Swanage was a fishing and quarrying town until its popularity as a holiday destination grew during the 19th century. Evidence of this development can still be seen in its   20 narrow streets and buildings constructed from local stone. These streets are home to a wide variety of pubs and restaurants to suit all visitors, from locally caught fish and chips to fine French cuisine. There are also many unusual shops selling fossils and gemstones, gifts, jewellery and art. Accommodation on offer ranges from camping, bed and breakfast, and self-catering holiday apartments, right up to five star luxury   25 hotels.

1. Which island can you see from Swanage in fine weather? Circle your answer.

   Isle of Wight   Emerald Isle   Isle of Black

2. What stands in the sea at the North end of the beach? Circle your answer.

   Old Henry Rocks   Old Harry Rocks   Old Harvey Rocks

3. Why has the Jurassic coastline been named a World Heritage site?

   _____

4. What is special about the squirrels on Brownsea Island?

   _____

5. What does the word *inspiration* mean in line 15?

   _____

6. What might keen walkers enjoy?

   _____

7–8. Before Swanage first became popular as a holiday destination, what two industries were people employed in?

   _____   _____

9. If you buy fish and chips, where will the fish have been caught?

   _____

10. Write a sentence describing what you would most enjoy about a trip to Swanage.

_____

_____ /10

Circle the words or phrases that have come into the English language in the past 100 years.

11–16. planet   microchip   mobile phone   book

website   spoon   MP3 player   oven

lamp   plasma TV   supermarket   wheel /6

Add the **suffix** *ful*, or *ish* to each word to make an **adjective**.

17. care _____   **18.** child _____

19. hope _____   **20.** sorrow _____

21. baby _____   **22.** fool _____ /6

Circle the correct **homophone** to complete each sentence.

23. I (mite might) be able to take piano lessons next year.

24. We are going to (see sea) a show at the theatre on Friday.

25. Sam (threw through) a ball for the kitten to chase.

26. I ate (to two) slices of pizza.

27. We (herd heard) a strange noise outside.

28. I need to (write right) a story about a castle. /6

Complete these **collective nouns**.

29. a _____ of sheep   **30.** a _____ of cows

31. a _____ of wolves   **32.** a _____ of grapes

33. a _____ of geese   **34.** a _____ of angels /6

Draw lines to match up each bold **verb** with a more powerful alternative.

35.	**walk**	leap
36.	**talk**	beam
37.	**run**	devour
38.	**smile**	saunter
39.	**jump**	sprint
40.	**eat**	chatter

/6

/40

PAPER 8

Dear Diary,

I'm writing this in my new bedroom. It smells of fresh paint and new carpet. This room is exactly how I wanted it. So why doesn't it feel like my room? It sounds really ungrateful, but I want my old room back. It was too small and the pink bunny wallpaper was embarrassing, but it felt like it was mine. This house feels too new, as if it is waiting for another family.

I've been thinking about Hannah and Sally, wondering what they're doing. They'll be at hockey practice tomorrow with the others. They'll probably have a match on Thursday. I don't even know if my new school has a hockey team. Still, I'll find out when I start tomorrow, I suppose.

My new uniform is hanging up on the back of the door. It's scratchy and uncomfortable. I hate the stripy tie and that green skirt is awful! Mum says that I have to give life here a chance; that it's bound to take time to settle in. I know it's hard for her too. She'll be stuck at home with Philip until she finds out about toddler groups for him. She had loads of friends before. Now she'll have to start again. Like me.

Hopefully tomorrow I'll be able to tell you about all my new friends. Maybe I'll get on the hockey team and perhaps my school skirt will look better on me than it does on the hanger!

Love Lucy x

1. What was on the wallpaper in Lucy's old bedroom? Circle your answer.

   puppies   ponies   bunnies

2. What does her new room smell like? Circle your answer.

   varnish and new curtains   fresh paint and new carpet   nail varnish and wood shavings

3–4. Write down two words used to describe how her new uniform feels.

   _____   _____

5. What advice does Lucy's mother give her?

   _____

6. Who is Phillip?

   _____

7. Why is Lucy thinking about her friends?

   _____

   _____

8–10. Write down three hopes that Lucy has for the next day.

   _____

   _____

   _____   /10

> Write down the **past tense** for each **present tense verb**.

11. speak _____   12. is _____

13. go _____   14. come _____

15. find _____   16. catch _____   /6

Choose a **full stop**, **question mark** or
exclamation mark to complete each sentence.

17. Do you know where Martin is ___

18. What a beautiful sunset___

19. Mr Monroe is so unfair___

20. The bus was late this morning___

21. Is that a new dress___

22. The boys grabbed their football and ran off___

/6

Add the correct **consonants** to complete
the names of different types of fruit.

23. _a _a _a   **24.** a _ _ e

25. o _ a _ _ e   **26.** _ i _ e a _ _ _ e

27. _ e a _   **28.** _ _ a _ e _

/6

Write down two more words that share the
bold letter string with each of these words.

29–30. night _____   _____

31–32. tear _____   _____

33–34. should** _____   _____

/6

Draw lines to separate the **syllables** in each word.

35. c o m p u t e r   36.   m a c h i n e r y

37. c u s h i o n   38.   h i p p o p o t a m u s

39. b a d g e r   40.   m i c r o s c o p e

/6

/40

PAPER 9

On with the show

Falling silently from leaden skies   1
With dancing, drifting clusters
of spiny webs,
winter takes a bow.

Beneath the crystal covering,   5
spring waits in the wings.
Chorus lines of snowdrops waiting
and it's on with the show.

Circle your answers.

1. What do you think is falling in the first verse of the poem?

    leaves   rain   snow

2. What colour is a *leaden sky* (line 1)?

    grey   blue   black

3. What are the *spiny webs* in line 3?

    raindrops   snowflakes   cobwebs

4–6. The poem says that winter takes a bow. Find three other places where the poem makes references to the theatre.

_____

_____

_____

7. What is the *crystal covering* in line 5?

_____

8. What are the *snowdrops* in line 7?

_____

/8

Circle the correct contracted form of the bold words.

9.	**are not**	are'nt	aren't
10.	**he is**	he's	hes'
11.	**they will**	they'll	theyl'l
12.	**should not**	shouldnt'	shouldn't
13.	**you are**	yo'are	you're
14.	**is not**	isn't	isnt'

/6

These words are homonyms. Write a sentence for each word, using a different meaning than before.

15. well _____

16. well _____

17. stamp _____

18. stamp _____

19. coach _____

20. coach _____

/6

Write down the feminine form of these words.

21. king _____   22. brother _____

23. father _____   24. duke _____

25. prince _____   26. uncle _____

/6

TALENT SHOW AUDITION

SINGER?

DANCER?

COMEDIAN?

CONJURER?

If you can do it, we want to see it!

Come to the school hall
at 12.30 on Friday

27. What is the poster advertising?

_____

28. What time is it taking place?

_____

29. What does the word *audition* mean?

_____

_____

30. Write down another word with a similar meaning to *conjurer*.

_____   /4

> Write down the **plurals** of these **singular nouns**.

31. box   _____   **32.** baby   _____

33. leaf   _____   **34.** beach   _____

35. wish   _____   **36.** hiss   _____   /6

> Write an interesting sentence about these topics.

37. Your favourite day of the week

_____

38. An activity you would like to try

_____

39. Your best memory

_____

40. Your first day at your school

_____   /4

/40

PAPER 10

Britain is a nation of chocolate-lovers, munching its way through around 10kg   1
per person each year. After Switzerland, Britain eats more chocolate than
anyone else. Most people are so used to chocolate that they are surprised to
discover that before the mid-1800s, solid eating chocolate did not exist at all.

The history of chocolate begins in South America, where the Maya and Aztec   5
civilisations developed a spicy drink made from roasted cocoa beans called
chocolatl. The drink was made from the beans of the cocoa tree which grew
wild in the Amazon basin. Cocoa beans were considered so valuable that as
well as being used to make the drink, the beans were used as currency by the
Maya. Four beans would buy a pumpkin and ten a rabbit.   10

After Europeans discovered Mexico during the 1500s, chocolate drinks quickly
became popular across Europe. From the mid-1600s chocolate houses began
opening in London, offering a range of chocolate drinks along with ale, beer and
snacks.

The first solid chocolate bars, for eating, appeared in the mid-1800s. They would   15
probably not be considered tasty by today's standards. At the same time, advances
in drinking chocolate production pressed out cocoa butter, which then became
available for use in solid chocolate. This made the chocolate tastier.

At first, only plain dark chocolate could be made, but a chocolate-maker from
Switzerland experimented with adding first powdered and then condensed   20
milk, resulting in a chocolate bar similar to what people might recognise today.

The range of chocolates available to buy seems to grow each year and the UK
now spends more than £3 billion a year on chocolate. Scientists are divided on
exactly why we love it so much, but chocolate seems to be here to stay.

1. Which nation eats the most chocolate? Circle your answer.

   Britain   France   Switzerland

2. What was the earliest chocolate drink called? Circle your answer.

   chocolatl   hotchoc   chocolade

3. What does the word *currency* (line 9) mean?

   _____

   _____

4–5. Write down two things, apart from chocolate drinks, that might have been served in
   a chocolate house.

   _____   _____

6. When did the first solid eating chocolate appear?

_____

7. What kind of butter made solid chocolate tastier?

_____

8. A chocolate-maker experimented with adding milk to the chocolate. Which country did he come from?

_____

9. How much do British people spend on chocolate each year?

_____

10. Write a sentence explaining why you do, or don't, like chocolate.

_____

_____

/10

Use these words to make six **compound words**. Use each word only once.

cup	pot	match	board	brush	lash
eye	stick	hair	foot	ball	tea

11. _____   **12.** _____

13. _____   **14.** _____

15. _____   **16.** _____

/6

Write down a **synonym** for these words.

17. angry _____   **18.** small _____

19. fast _____   **20.** sad _____

21. wet _____   **22.** neat _____

/6

Turn these words into **verbs** by adding the **suffix** *en* or *ise*.

23. real_____   **24.** critic_____   **25.** deep_____

26. special_____   **27.** weak_____   **28.** deaf_____

/6

Add *its* or *it's* to complete each sentence.

29. The boat broke clear of _____ moorings.

30. Mum is trying to mend the vase because _____ broken.

31. Our beech tree drops _____ leaves in the autumn.

32. Dad will call us when _____ time for tea.

33. I like maths but _____ hard sometimes.

34. A snake sheds _____ skin as it grows.

/6

Label these sentences **a-f** to arrange them in the right order.

35. _____ We looked everywhere for her.

36. _____ Our dog went missing.

37. _____ Next, the people who found her saw our posters.

38. _____ When we could not find her, we put up posters in our town.

39. _____ Meanwhile, someone had found our dog.

40. _____ Finally, the people brought our dog back to us.

/6

/40

PAPER 11

Wood Lane Primary School Debating Society
Should people be allowed to wear real fur?

"I believe that it is wrong to kill animals just so that we can wear their fur. Animals that are farmed or caught for their fur suffer terribly and there is no need for it to happen. Modern artificial fur looks and feels just like the real thing and it can be made without causing animals to suffer.

Fur is used mainly for fashion, rather than to keep warm, and in any case there are lots of other warm materials we can use to make clothes, like wool and man-made fleece fabrics.

If people stopped buying clothes made with real fur, then the fur trade would disappear completely.

That is why I think people should not wear real fur. Please vote for me, Sam, in the debate."

———————————

"My name is Nina. I believe that there is nothing wrong with wearing animal fur. People have kept warm using fur for thousands of years. Real fur is very warm and beautiful to look at. If people can afford to buy it, why shouldn't they be able to?

Most of us eat meat and I don't see the difference between farming animals for food and farming them for fur.

Also, lots of people have jobs in the fur trade and in the fashion industry. If nobody wore fur these people would have no jobs.

That is why I think people should be able to wear real fur if they want to. Please vote for me in this debate."

1–2. Write down two reasons why Sam thinks that artificial fur is a good idea.

_____

_____

3–4. List two things he suggests we could use instead of fur, to make warm clothes.

_____

_____

5. What does he argue would happen to the fur trade if people stopped buying real fur?

_____

6–7. Write down two advantages of real fur that Nina mentions.

_____

_____

8. In your own words, explain Nina's point about farming for meat and farming for fur.

_____

_____

9–10. Who would you vote for in this debate? Give at least two reasons for your answer.

_____

_____

/10

Write an **antonym** for each word.

11. early _____

12. buy _____

13. float _____

14. hard _____

15. narrow _____

16. first _____

/6

Draw lines to link each word with its **definition**.

17. done with speed   careless

18. full of happiness   really

19. done without attention   graceful

20. genuinely   penniless

21. without money   rapidly

22. moving beautifully   joyful

/6

Write each word in the chart, according to its **prefix**.

23–28. cooperate   misbehave   mistrust   export

coordinate   exchange

mis	co	ex

/6

Add the missing **commas** to each sentence.

29–30. Jack plays cricket football rugby and tennis.

31–32. I have been to Greece Spain France and Italy on holiday.

33. On Saturday Jessica had to clean her room walk the dog and play with her hamster.

34–35. We ordered dough balls pizza garlic bread and salad for lunch.

/7

Write these words again in **alphabetical order**.

house   hoard   hound   hour   hoist

36. _____

37. _____

38. _____

39. _____

40. _____

/5

/40

PAPER 12

Witness report

It must have been about 12.15pm. I was standing by the lion enclosure with my family. There were lots of people there because the keepers were about to feed the lions.

Some people made room for me so that I could get closer to the wire to see the lions being fed. I could see the keepers opening the gate in the outer fence. They both went inside and closed the gate. I couldn't see whether they locked it again.

The keepers took a large padlock off a small hatch in the inner fence. It wouldn't have been big enough for an adult lion to fit through because even the piece of meat got stuck. The keepers pushed and shoved it and then one of the lions came and started pulling at the meat from inside the enclosure. That must have loosened it because the meat suddenly shot into the enclosure. Two of the adult lionesses started eating the meat straight away and their cubs hung about hoping to get some meat too.

One keeper had started to leave through the outer fence before the other one had closed the hatch. He was watching the lions feeding so he didn't notice that one of the cubs had sneaked up to the hatch and was squeezing through. He dashed through the gate in the outer fence before the keeper could close it.

A few people started to panic and run away but most stayed to watch. The lion seemed curious about people and was running from person to person to have a closer look. The keepers called out, "Stay calm. Don't run or you will scare him."

Suddenly a different keeper dashed up with a large, strong net. I couldn't see what happened next because there were people in the way. I could hear the cub snarling and growling and then I saw it back in the cage with the other lions.

Answer these questions.

1. What time of day does the event happen? Circle your answer.

12.15am   12.45am   12.15pm

2. Why does the witness get such a good view of what happened?

_____

_____

Answer booklet English 8–9

Paper 1

1. maths
2. cheese spread
3. Max
4. with coloured chalk on black paper
5. it was rainy
6–7. Joe is writing a story about the autumn.
8. He is making a firework picture and bonfire night takes place in autumn.
9. I would feel surprised and a bit scared.
10. It means to breathe in sharply in surprise or fear.
11. Because he never expected to see a pair of eyes down a drain.
11. green
12. happy
13. huge
14. dark
15. frosty
16. soft
17. candle
18. table
19. cradle
20. bottle
21. stable
22. ankle
23. unhappy
24. disqualify
25. disappear
26. unfair
27. unpack
28. disagree
29–30. door   bell
31–32. cheese   cake
33–34. ear   ring
35. blue
36. green
37. orange
38. pink
39. purple
40. red

Paper 2

1. Europe
2. Because oases have water.
3–5. Any three of the following: Egypt, Libya, Morocco, Chad, Tunisia
6. Because fossils have been found.
7. a hill of sand
8–9. large, flat feet for walking on sand; long eyelashes to keep sound out of their eyes.
10. Because it gets very cold in the desert at night.
11. saw
12. right
13. tap
14. ball
15. train
16. light
17. eggs
18. dishes
19. gloves
20. witches
21. buses
22. zoos
23. The girl climbed the stairs.
24. Flowers grow in the park.
25. A flock of birds flew over our garden.
26. My brother plays basketball for his school.
27. The cat balanced on the fence.
28. Sarah wandered slowly to school.

29–34. pillow, rabbit, fortune, follow, candle, bubble
35. kindly
36. hopeful
37. forgetful
38. actually
39. likely
40. painful

Paper 3

1. to extend the school
2. The buildings were not big enough.
3–4. Because Emily will have to walk for a long time to reach school. Because she will have to cross three major roads.
5. Because they were crumbling.
6–7. Roads will become busier with parents driving to the school. Traffic-calming measures will slow down local traffic.
8. speed bumps
9. Harris Homes
10. In a win-win situation, everybody is better off, so both the schoolchildren and the tax-payers will benefit.
11. there
12. There
13. their
14. there
15. their
16. their
17. low
18. small
19. found
20. full
21. dirty
22. short
23. Ben walked to school.
24. The girls collected shells on the beach.
25. I wished by the wishing well.
26. Mum baked cherry cakes.
27. I switched on the lights at night time.
28. Sally brushed her long hair.
29. table
30. bubble
31. carry
32. happy
33. pepper
34. summer
35. I am
36. she will
37. could not
38. they are
39. he is
40. we will

Paper 4

1. plain
2. flour
3. decoration
4. a flavouring that is not man-made
5. The small amount of salt that can be picked up between the thumb and forefinger.
6. Because it has a golden colour.
7. So the biscuits will not stick.
8. the different foods you mix to make gingerbread men
9. the bowls, spoons, tins etc you need to make gingerbread men
10. biscuit tin
11. France

12. October
13. Monday
14. Sally
15. Europe
16. Liam
17. am
18. is
19. am
20. are
21. are
22. is
23. We were late because the alarm clock was broken.
24. Dad was delighted because he won the football match.
25. Mum made us pizza for tea.
26. I would love to go rock climbing.
27. You must cross the road carefully.
28. Mum and Dad are grumpy when they wake up in the morning.
29. ancient
30. sea
31. concerned
32. street
33. reply
34. home
35. export
36. hopeful
37. heroic
38. winner
39. golden
40. realistic

Paper 5

1. fairytales
2–3. crooked, rickety
4. rotting
5. Because the house is spooky and unusual and they want to know who is living there.
6–7. creaky, squeaky
8. There are bugs in her hair.
9. She was about to have dinner.
10. She wants to put the children in her soup.
11-16. camel, come, giant, grape, sausage, soil
17-22. First, Grandad filled little pots with compost, before using a pencil to make a little hole in the soil. Next, he dropped a seed into each hole, then gently covered the seed with compost. After that, he watered each pot carefully and finally placed them on the windowsill in the sunlight.
23. childhood
24. knighthood
25. friendship
26. boyhood
27. ownership
28. neighbourhood
29. partnership
30. membership
31. "What a beautiful picture!" said the teacher.
32. Dad called up the stairs, "Have you seen my keys?"
33. Poppy shouted, "Great goal!"
34. "We'll be late if we don't hurry!" warned Mum.
35. the dog's paw
36. the woman's car
37. a cat's tail
38. the girl's foot
39. a town's roads
40. the boy's nose

Paper 6

1. monkey
2. kuyu
3. Because he is sick of eating salty fish.
4–5. crafty, puzzled
6. king
7. He is afraid because he knows that the shark wants his heart.
8. He tells the shark that he left his heart in a tree at home so he needs to go back and get it.
9. 9 days
10. I think the monkey is wiser because he manages to trick the shark into taking him home safely.
11. Anna wrote as neatly as she could, not smudging the ink at all.
12. Tail wagging wildly, the puppy chased the ball.
13. Not finding any boots she liked, Nina bought some shoes instead.
14. When nobody answered the phone, Max left a message.
15. kindly
16. prettily
17. actually
18. daintily
19. fully
20. dizzily
21. rudely
22. gracefully
23. Mark
24. 3
25. Paulo
26. Because he is the oldest.
27. piglet
28. duckling
29. gosling
30. kitten
31. signet
32. foal
33. cub
34. joey
35. while
36. when
37. because
38. so
39. but
40. before

Paper 7

1. Isle of Wight
2. Old Harry Rocks
3. because of its geology
4. they are rare red squirrels
5. a thing that gives someone the idea for something
6. miles of cliff-top walks
7–8. fishing, quarrying
9. in the sea off Swanage
10. Answers will vary.
11–16. microchip, mobile phone, MP3 player, website, plasma TV, supermarket
17. careful
18. childish
19. hopeful
20. sorrowful
21. babyish
22. foolish
23. might
24. see
25. threw
26. two
27. heard
28. write
29. flock

30. herd
31. pack
32. bunch
33. gaggle
34. host
35. saunter
36. chatter
37. sprint
38. beam
39. leap
40. devour

Paper 8

1. bunnies
2. fresh paint and new carpet
3–4. scratchy, uncomfortable
5. She advises her to give life there a chance.
6. Lucy's younger brother
7. Because they have moved house.
8–10. to make new friends; to get on the hockey team; that her skirt will look better on her than on the hanger
11. spoke
12. was
13. went
14. came
15. found
16. caught
17. ?
18. !
19. !
20. .
21. ?
22. .
23. banana
24. apple
25. orange
26. pineapple
27. pear
28. grapes
29–34. Possible answers include:
29–30. tight, fright
31–32. fear, year
33–34. could, would
35. com/pu/ter
36. mach/in/er/y
37. cush/ion
38. hipp/o/pot/am/us
39. badg/er
40. mi/cro/scope

Paper 9

1. snow
2. grey
3. snowflakes
4–6. spring waits in the wings, chorus lines, on with the show
7. snow
8. flowers
9. aren't
10. he's
11. they'll
12. shouldn't
13. you're
14. isn't
15–20. Answers will vary.
21. queen
22. sister
23. mother
24. duchess
25. princess
26. aunt
27. a talent show
28. 12.30pm
29. An event where people show what they can do to see if they are good enough to enter the talent show.

30. magician
31. boxes
32. babies
33. leaves
34. beaches
35. wishes
36. hisses
37–40. Answers will vary.

Paper 10

1. Switzerland
2. chocolatl
3. money
4–5. Any two from: ale, beer, snacks
6. mid-1800s
7. cocoa butter
8. Switzerland
9. £3 billion
10. Answers will vary.
11. cupboard
12. eyelash
13. matchstick
14. football
15. teapot
16. hairbrush
17–22. Possible answers include:
17. cross
18. tiny
19. quick
20. unhappy
21. damp
22. tidy
23. realise
24. criticise
25. deepen
26. specialise
27. weaken
28. deafen
29. its
30. it's
31. its
32. it's
33. it's
34. its
35–40. b, a, e, c, d, f

Paper 11

1–2. it looks like the real thing, it can be made without harming animals
3–4. wool, man-made fleece fabric
5. it would disappear
6–7. it is very warm, it looks beautiful
8. she argues that there is no difference between farming animals for meat and farming them for fur
9–10. Answers will vary.
11–16. Possible answers include:
11. late
12. sell
13. sink
14. soft/easy
15. wide
16. last
17. rapidly
18. joyful
19. careless
20. really
21. penniless
22. graceful
23–28.

mis	co	ex
misbehave	cooperate	export
mistrust	coordinate	exchange

29–30. Jack plays cricket, football, rugby and tennis.
31–32. I have been to Greece, Spain, France and Italy on holiday.

2

33. On Saturday Jessica had to walk the dog, clean out the rabbits and play with her hamster.

34–35. We ordered dough balls, pizza, garlic bread and salad for lunch.

36–40. hoard, hoist, hound, hour, house

Paper 12

1. 12.15pm
2. Adults made room for them so they could see the lions being fed.
3. the meat got stuck in the hatch
4–5. They leave the hatch open, one keeper opens the outer gate before the hatch is closed.
6. An adult lion could not have escaped because the hatch was too small.
7. The cub was not dangerous because most people are not afraid of it and the keepers were worried that the people would scare the cub, not that the cub would harm the people.
8–9. whether the keeper locked the gate; how the cub got back into the cage
10. The lion cub was caught by the keeper in the net and put back in the cage.
11. five boys' test papers
12. the girl's bag
13. six birds' wings
14. three dogs' tails
15. the five teachers' desks
16. three cars' engines
17. although
18. so
19. but
20. and
21. if
22. because

23–28.

common nouns	proper nouns
mouse	Paris
week	Christmas
class	Jennifer

29. A <u>large, black</u> cat was curled up on the chair.
30. The cake was smothered with <u>sweet, sticky, pink</u> icing.
31. Laura's hair, <u>tangled and windswept</u>, stood out in all directions.
32. We left footprints in the <u>cold, crisp, white</u> snow.
33. Luke rode by on his <u>blue, shiny new</u> bike.
34. The garden was full of <u>bright, colourful</u> flowers.
35. though
36. twice
37. shout
38. sausage
39. earn
40. height

Paper 13

1. school
2. They didn't like the school food.
3. sports socks and sweaty trainers
4. Jack
5. Because they can do it later or Mum might do them with the dinner things.
6. Because she is tired from work.
7. Because it is her birthday cake.

8. Ben
9–10. Answers will vary.
11. better
12. darker
13. neater
14. quicker
15. sweeter
16. warmer
17–20. Possible answers include: ceiling, receive, circle, circus
21–22. Answers will vary.
23. hoping
24. dinner
25. bitter
26. lady
27. tapping
28. supper
29. "Hurry up!" called Mum.
30. "Where are my hockey boots?" asked Saffron.
31. "Does everyone have enough to eat?" asked Dad.
32. "That tickles!" giggled Sophie.
33. "Get out of my room!" shouted Mark, angrily.
34. "Which way is the swimming pool?" asked Lucy.
35. environment
36. statement
37. fitness
38. government
39. kindness
40. illness

Paper 14

1. 20 minutes
2. the footpath is narrow
3. 10 minutes
4. The shop sells great sweets.
5–6. footbridge, zebra crossing
7. blue
8. reserved for people walking
9. 3.00pm
10. to play football
11–16. sheep, fish, aircraft, buffalo, salmon, traffic
17–22. Answers will vary.
23. weakling
24. droplet
25. bracelet
26. sapling
27. leaflet
28. dumpling
29–30. I scored four goals for our team.
31–32. Sam knew straight away that he would like the new boy.
33–34. Chloe ran inside because she did not want to be stung by the bee.
35–36. I would love to stay up late but I know that Mum will say no.
37–40. Poppy likes dogs.
Sally doesn't like drawing pictures.
Poppy does not like playing netball.
Sally enjoys PE lessons.

Paper 15

1. A song that sends people to sleep.
2–3. Barney is a dog. He has fur, and he does not like cats.
4. Because it is raining.
5. to the farm
6. Because none of the boxes smelled of food.
7. sausages
8. the sound of sausages cooking
9. breakfast time
10. He is about to steal the sausages.
11. promotion

12. translation
13. reaction
14. creation
15. education
16. conclusion
17. My friend kept chickens.
18. I could ice skate really well.
19. I saw my grandparents every weekend.
20. Faith wrote secrets in her diary.
21. I bought a magazine each Friday.
22. I ran faster than anyone else in my class.
23. we're
24. I'll
25. they're
26. you've
27. it'll
28. would've
29. he
30. them
31. we
32. they
33. us
34. me
35–37. Answers will vary.
38–40. Answers will vary.

Paper 16

1. distant or isolated
2. By charging each other less than they should.
3. A violent storm blew up.
4. The door had blown in and half of the roof had gone.
5. Because he had just made a lot of money selling his work, so he didn't need to work any more.
6. Because he had been helping people who couldn't afford to pay him.
7. Their houses are cold and damp.
8. The carpenter could have prevented some people from becoming ill by fixing their houses so that they were not cold and damp.
9. The fact that the carpenter can pay will not make a difference to how quickly his son is treated because the doctor does not mind whether or not his patients can pay him.
10. The carpenter became greedy when he became rich, so he wouldn't help his neighbours any more.
11. sword
12. woman
13. wolf
14. wool
15. worm
16. two
17–20. Possible answers include:
17. I clambered over the slippery rocks at the foot of the cliff.
18. Paul dozed restlessly in the chair by the fire.
19. Maria gazed out of the window at the view.
20. Peter smashed the piggy bank to see what was inside.
21–28.

phone	oct	vent	press
telephone	octopus	invent	pressure
megaphone	octagon	prevent	impress

29. pitiful
30. running

31. daring
32. stylish
33. beautiful
34. childish
35. bull
36. drake
37. grandfather
38. nephew
39. lady
40. husband

Paper 17
1. a shopping centre
2. 10
3. 9.00am
4–5. Any two of: jugglers, acrobats, stilt walkers
6. No, some are worried about the roads around the centre.
7. Disruption means something that interferes with or spoils the normal routine.
8. To make up for the inconvenience the people of the town have had to put up with.
9. a digger which damaged gas pipes and a water main
10. Because they are worried that the new car park will not be big enough for the extra traffic.
11–15. Possible answers include:
11. kitchen
12. It
13. sauntered
14. dewy
15. lightly
16. its
17. It's
18. it's
19. its
20. its

ible	able
edible	reliable
horrible	adorable
possible	enjoyable
responsible	valuable

21–28.
29–30. Our cat, who hates water, got soaked in the rain.
31. Running for the bus, I tripped and fell.
32–33. On the school trip we tried canoeing, abseiling, climbing and raft-building.
34. After a good wash, the car looked like new.
35. I needed to buy flour, sugar and eggs to make the cake.
36. left
37. fair
38. wave
39. jam
40. book

Paper 18
1. sofa
2. 2
3. It was the wrong colour.
4. Because young children can make a mess.
5. Because it does not match the rest of his furniture.
6. He rang the store to complain.
7. No, because they only wanted to buy one beige sofa and the mistake is not their fault.

8–9. disappointed, angry
10. He wants a full refund.
11–18.

add er	add est
taller	tallest
bigger	biggest
hotter	hottest
shorter	shortest

19–22. Answers will vary.
23. transatlantic
24. telephone
25. television
26. transparent
27. translate
28. telescope
29–34. Possible answers include:
29. cough
30. near
31. soup
32. launch
33. spice
34. wait
35–40. Possible answers include:
35. We relaxed in the warm sun.
36. Pippa is terrified of the dark.
37. The old house was spooky.
38. We chose a huge Christmas tree.
39. Dad was furious because I was late home.
40. It was chilly last night.

Paper 19
1. she does
2. 3
3. No, because he had only seen cows in pictures and has come from London.
4. jostled
5. He could be crushed between two cows or trampled beneath their hooves
6. She means that they will be gentle because lambs are gentle.
7–8. grass-scented sighs; air smelt fresh and clear
9. Because they were not safe in the air-raids in London.
10. during World War II
11. autograph
12. automobile
13. bicycle
14. bifocal
15. autobiography
16. bilingual
17. bimonthly
18. autopilot
19–22. Landing in Egypt, we couldn't believe how hot it was.
23–28. Possible answers include:
23. valuable
24. in the end
25. the letters of the alphabet except a,e,i,o and u
26. having courage
27. nearby
28. a room or building containing many books
29–34. Sentences will vary.
35–40. Possible answers include:
35. handbag
36. railway
37. airport
38. motorbike
39. windmill
40. playground

Paper 20
1. a holiday which combines a cruise with a stay in a hotel
2. A trip to visit a place or attraction.
3–4. Any two of: Valley of the Kings, Luxor Temple, Karnak Temple, Aswan High Dam
5. So that they can speak Egyptian to local Egyptians and also answer the questions of English-speaking guests.
6. Because Egypt is a hot country.
7–8. Any two of: Luxor Museum, sound and light show, Colossi of Memnon
9. To save them from being flooded during the construction of the Aswan Dam.
10. No, unlimited use of the spa is included in the price.
11. stationary
12. personal
13. atomic
14. realistic
15. dictionary
16. seasonal
17–32. Possible answers include:
17–18. curious, serious
19–20. social, artificial
21–22. rough, though
23–28. Possible answers include:
23. The storm was approaching rapidly so we walked more quickly towards home.
24. The funny clown told us a hilarious joke.
25. John is unkind to the younger children and mean to his sister.
26. I cut up an onion while Dad chopped a pepper to go in the chilli.
27. Jenny was happy with her present and Max was delighted with his.
28. The pretty princess had beautiful hair.
29–34. Possible answers include:

29.	a sunset	fiery golden ball
30.	a lion	ferocious predator
31.	a traffic jam	winding into the distance like a snake
32.	a waterfall	a wall of shimmering water
33.	a beach	a sandy strip, yellow against the blue sea
34.	a roller coaster	a winding framework curling like metallic ribbon

35–40. Possible answers include:
35. "Your picture is great!" said Mark, admiringly.
36. The stars twinkled brightly in the inky sky.
37. The boys gobbled up the chips hungrily.
38. I wrote the answers neatly on the test paper.
39. "Hello!" called the twins, cheerfully.
40. James built the model ship carefully.

3. What happened to the meat when the keepers tried to feed the lions?

_____

_____

4–5. List two mistakes that the keepers made that allowed the cub to escape.

_____

_____

6. Would it have been possible for an adult lion to escape in the same way? Give a reason for your answer.

_____

_____

7. Do you think the cub was dangerous? Use evidence from the text to support your answer.

_____

_____

8–9. List two things in the statement that the witness doesn't see clearly.

_____

_____

10. How do you think the lion cub got back into the cage?

_____

_____ **/10**

Add the **apostrophe** in the correct place.

11. five boys test papers

12. the girls bag

13. six birds wings

14. three dogs tails

15. the five teachers desks

16. three cars engines

/6

Choose a suitable **conjunction** from the box to complete each sentence.

and   although   because   if   so   but

17. Katie shared her lunch ＿＿＿＿＿＿ she was hungry.

18. I worked hard ＿＿＿＿＿＿ I would do well in my test.

19. I loved the shoes ＿＿＿＿＿＿ the shop did not have them in my size.

20. I passed the ball to Nick ＿＿＿＿＿＿ he scored a goal.

21. I can watch my favourite TV programme ＿＿＿＿＿＿ I finish my homework in time.

22. Mum was angry ＿＿＿＿＿＿ my room was in a mess.

/6

Complete this table by sorting these words into **common nouns** and **proper nouns.**

Paris   mouse   Christmas   week   Jennifer   class

23–28.

common nouns	proper nouns

/6

Underline the **adjectival phrase** in each sentence.

29. A large, black cat was curled up on the chair.

30. The cake was smothered with sweet, sticky, pink icing.

31. Laura's hair, tangled and wind-swept, stood out in all directions.

32. We left footprints in the cold, crisp, white snow.

33. Luke rode by on his blue, shiny, new bike.

34. The garden was full of bright, colourful flowers.

/6

> Draw lines to match up the pairs of words that
> have the same letter string but a different sound.

35.	**c**ough	shout
36.	not**ice**	sausage
37.	f**ou**r	though
38.	**au**nt	height
39.	h**ear**	twice
40.	w**eight**	earn

/6

/40

PAPER 13

Scene 2

Jack and Ben come in from school. They are in the kitchen. Jack opens the fridge door.

Ben: I'm starving!

Jack: Me too! That pasta bake at lunchtime was disgusting.
          What do they put in school food?

Ben: I reckon they boil up all the sports socks and sweaty trainers in lost property! Hey
          do you want some of this cake?

Ben takes out a chocolate cake on a plate.

Jack: Do you think we should?

Ben: Oh come on! It's only a cake. I'm having some, even if you don't.

Jack: Oh go on then, just a small bit.

The boys quickly eat all of the cake.

Jack: We'd better wash up these plates.

Ben: No, don't worry about it. We'll do it later. If we're lucky, Mum'll do them with the dinner plates. No sense making work for ourselves.

The boys leave as Mum comes in from work. She is carrying heavy shopping and looks tired.

Mum: Hello boys. Good day?

Ben calls from offstage: It was OK mum.

Mum: (*angrily*) Ben, Jack, come here!

Mum is holding up the cake plate as the boys come into the kitchen

Mum: What's this?

Ben: We were hungry.

Jack: We were going to wash up the plates, honest!

Mum: That was my birthday cake! You've eaten the whole thing!

1. Where have the boys come in from? Circle your answer.

   a football match   the shops   school

2. Why are they hungry? Circle your answer.

   they forgot their   they didn't like   they didn't eat
   packed lunch   the school food   any breakfast

3. What does Ben think they put in the school food?

   _____

4. Who isn't sure whether they should eat the cake?

   _____

5. Why does Ben say they shouldn't wash up the plates?

   _____

   _____

6. Why might Mum not be in a very good mood, even before she sees the cake plates?

   _____

   _____

7. Why do you think Mum is angry about the cake?

_____

_____

8. Which of the two boys do you think has behaved the worst?

_____

_____

9–10. Write down two things you might happen in the next scene?

_____

_____

_____ **/10**

Find and underline an **adjective** in each sentence that ends with *er*.

11. I want my project to be better than my last one.

12. Now that is it autumn, the evenings are much darker.

13. My homework is neater than I have managed before.

14. Dan ran the race quicker than the rest of the team.

15. Adding sugar to teak makes it taste sweeter.

16. I changed my thin jacket for a warmer coat. **/6**

Write down four words which contain a soft *c*, e.g. cinema

17. _____   **18.** _____

19. _____   **20.** _____   **/4**

Choose two of your words and write a sentence containing each one.

21. _____

22. _____ **/2**

Underline the correct word in each set of brackets to complete the sentences.

23. I am (hoping hopping) to get a guitar for my birthday.

24. Mum and Dad love holding (diner dinner) parties.

25. We don't eat orange peel because it is (biter bitter).

26. I stood up on the bus to let an old (lady laddy) sit down.

27. The tree branch was (taping tapping) against my bedroom window.

28. We had cheese on toast for (supper super).

/6

Add the **speech marks** to these sentences.

29. Hurry up! called Mum.

30. Where are my hockey boots? asked Saffron.

31. Does everyone have enough to eat? asked Dad.

32. That tickles! giggled Sophie.

33. Get out of my room! shouted Mark, angrily.

34. Which way is the swimming pool? asked Lucy.

/6

Add the **suffix** *ness* or *ment* to each word.

35. environ_____

36. state_____

37. fit_____

38. govern_____

39. kind_____

40. ill_____

/6

/40

PAPER 14

Dear Harry

I am very glad you can come and play for the team at the weekend. If your parents can't drop you off, it only takes 20 minutes to walk from your house. Here are the directions.

Turn right out of your gate. Walk to the end of your road, then turn right again into Boundary Road. Half way down, cross at the zebra crossing and turn into Mill Lane. The pavement is rather narrow so be careful if there is a lot of traffic.

When you get to the end of Mill Lane there is a public footpath. It is a short-cut through to Albion Road which should save you 10 minutes. At the end of the footpath turn left along Albion Road until you get to a corner with a sweet shop. (Bring some money because this shop sells great sweets!)

After the sweet shop, cross the side-road and carry on along Albion Road until it joins Church Street. This is a very busy road so carry on until you get to the footbridge and cross there. Look for a blue house. There's a path between it and the neighbouring house that will bring you out by the shopping centre. This whole area is pedestrianised so you don't need to worry about traffic!

I'm sure you know how to get to the park from there. It's about five minutes walk down the High Street, then left by the baker shop.

I'll be there from about 3pm and kick-off is at 3.30pm. Don't forget your footie boots!

See you on Saturday,

Jacob

Circle your answers.

1. How long should it take Harry to walk to the park?

10 minutes   25 minutes   20 minutes

2. Why should Harry be careful in Mill Lane?

the road is busy   the footpath is narrow   a fierce dog lives there

3. Jacob suggests a short cut through to Albion Road. How much time should that save Harry?

10 minutes   20 minutes   5 minutes

Answer these questions.

4. Why does Jacob suggest that Harry should bring some money?

_____

5–6. List two different ways mentioned in the directions to cross roads safely.

_____

_____

7. What colour is the house Jacob should look for?

_____

8. If a pedestrian is someone walking rather than driving, what do you think the word *pedestrianised* means?

_____

_____

9. What time will Jacob be at the park on Saturday?

_____

10. Why are they meeting at the park?

_____   /10

Circle the words which do not change in the **plural**.

11–16.   sheep   mouse   kite   fish   aircraft   cow

    buffalo   salmon   kitten   traffic   house   nation   /6

Write a sentence containing each **verb** and **adverb** pair.

17. walked quickly

_____

18. walked slowly

_____

19. sang beautifully

_____

20. sang terribly

_____

21. worked carefully

_____

22. worked carelessly

_____

/6

Add _ling_ or _let_ to each word to make a **diminutive**.

23. weak_____   **24.** drop_____   **25.** brace_____

26. sap_____   **27.** leaf_____   **28.** dump_____

/6

Put the pairs of **homophones** in the correct place in each sentence.

29–30. I scored _____ goals _____ our team. (for four)

31–32. Sam _____ straight away that he would like the _____ boy. (knew new)

33–34. Chloe ran inside because she did not want to _____ stung by the _____.
(bee be)

35–36. I would love to stay up late but I _____ that Mum will say _____.
(no know)

/8

Read the text, then underline the sentences that are true.

Poppy has a brother. She loves all animals, drawing pictures and writing stories. She doesn't like any sport.

Sally has two sisters. She is good at gymnastics and loves going to parties. She doesn't like art.

37–40. Poppy likes dogs.   Sally has a brother.

Sally doesn't like drawing pictures.   Poppy has two sisters.

Poppy does not like playing netball.   Sally enjoys PE lessons.

/4

/40

PAPER 15

The steady sound of the train worked like a lullaby on Barney. When he woke up, he could see pinpricks of daylight around the edge of the carriage door. He felt the train slow down, and heard voices outside. The door slid open and faces peered in.

Barney didn't wait to find out whether they were friendly or not. Growling, he leapt off the train and ran. Hearing the train pull out the station behind him and pick up speed, Barney decided he was safe for now. He slowed to a trot.

It had started to rain heavily and Barney's fur was wet through. Shaking himself briskly, Barney looked around for a place to shelter. There were houses up ahead and one had an old garage at the front. It didn't look very cosy, or very safe for that matter, but the door was open a little and Barney crept inside.

Out of the rain, Barney had time to think. In this weather, finding drinking water wouldn't be a problem but he'd had nothing to eat since the previous morning. If he was going to find his way back to his farm he would need to find some food first. He looked around him. The garage was full of cardboard boxes. Some had old car parts sticking out of the top. Others were sealed shut with thick brown tape. None of them smelled of food but at least there was no sign of any cats.

Barney ventured out of the garage. A delicious smell wafted past him. Sausages! Barney followed the smell around the back of the garage and along a winding path to the back of the house. The kitchen door was open and Barney could hear sizzling from inside. Mouth watering, Barney crept up to the back door and peered inside. There was the cooker and there was the frying pan. Judging by the smell coming from the pan, the food was nearly ready. Best of all, there was nobody guarding his breakfast!

1

5

10

15

20

Answer these questions.

1. What does the word *lullaby* (line 1) mean?

_____

2–3 Who or what do you think Barney is? Give two pieces of evidence from the text to explain how you know.

_____

_____

4. Why wouldn't it be a problem for Barney to find drinking water?

_____

5. Where is Barney trying to get back to?

_____

6. How did Barney know there was no food in the garage?

_____

7. What can Barney smell when he leaves the garage?

_____

8. What is the sizzling sound that Barney can hear?

_____

9. What time of day is it in the story?

_____

10. What is Barney about to do when the story extract ends?

_____   /10

Add the **suffix** *ion* to each word. You may need to alter the spelling of the word slightly first.

11. promote + ion =   _____

12. translate + ion =   _____

13. react + ion =   _____

14. create + ion =   _____

15. educate + ion =   _____

16. conclude + ion =   _____   /6

Write these sentences again in the **past tense**.

17. My friend keeps chickens.

_____

18. I can ice skate really well.

_____

19. I see my grandparents every weekend.

_____

20. Faith writes secrets in her diary.

_____

21. I buy a magazine each Friday.

_____

22. I run faster than anyone else in my class.

_____ /6

Write these pairs of words as **contractions**.

23. we are _____   **24.** I will _____

25. they are _____   **26.** you have _____

27. it will _____   **28.** would have _____ /6

Add a suitable **personal pronoun** to complete each sentence.

29. Dad hunted high and low because _____ could not find his car keys.

30. My friends are coming over later so I can help _____ with their homework.

31. My brother and I brushed our teeth because _____ were going to the dentist.

32. My cousins like coming to stay because _____ love exploring the city.

33. It was cold playing in the snow so Mum made _____ some hot chocolate.

34. My auntie bought _____ a new outfit for my birthday.

/6

Write a sentence to match each sentence ending.

35. _____ ?

36. _____ !

37. _____ .

/3

Write an **adjectival phrase** to describe these things.

38. a snowy scene _____

39. fireworks _____

40. a beach _____

/3

/40

PAPER 16

The proud carpenter

Many years ago there lived a poor carpenter. He worked hard and his work was   1
good but the people in his remote village never had enough money to pay him,
so he always charged them less than he should. The villagers all helped each
other in this way. All were good workers who charged less than they could, to
help their neighbours.   5

One day, a rich merchant passed through the village. He admired the carpenter's
beautiful work so much that he offered to buy it all, at a very high price. The
delighted carpenter agreed and sat down to count his money.

That night a violent storm blew up. Many of the village houses were damaged. At first light the carpenter's neighbour, who was a doctor, knocked at his door. 10

"My door has blown in and half of my roof has gone," he said. "Please help me."

The carpenter remembered the praise of the merchant and the pile of money he had paid.

"What can you pay me?" asked the carpenter.

"My friend, I have no money," he replied. "When people are sick I try to heal them 15 but nobody has money to pay me. You know how it is."

The carpenter grew angry. "I am a great carpenter. Yesterday I sold all of my work at a high price. If you can't pay me then I won't help you."

Throughout the day, other neighbours came to ask the carpenter for help. Each time he sent them away with the same message. Some time later, the carpenter's son became 20 very ill. The carpenter immediately called on his neighbour, the doctor. His wife answered the door.

"I'm sorry," she said. "Since the storm, the villagers' damaged homes are cold and damp. Their children are sick. My husband is trying to heal them."

"But I can pay!" argued the carpenter. 25

The doctor's wife shrugged. "When he gets back I'll tell him you called, but he's very busy. You know how it is."

1. What is the meaning of the word *remote* (line 2)?

_____

2. How did the villagers manage to buy what they needed from each other?

_____

3. A rich merchant bought the carpenter's work. What happened to the village that night?

_____

_____

4. What damage was done to the house of the carpenter's neighbour?

_____

_____

5. Explain in your own words why the carpenter would not help.

_____

_____

6. Why couldn't the doctor pay for the repairs to his house?

_____

_____

7. Some time later, more people in the village become ill. What reason does the doctor's wife give for this?

_____

_____

8. Do you think that the carpenter could have prevented some of the villagers from becoming ill? Give a reason for your answer.

_____

_____

9. Do you think the fact that the carpenter can pay the doctor will make a difference to how quickly his son is treated? Give a reason for your answer.

_____

_____

10. What do you think was the main mistake the carpenter made?

_____

_____ /10

Write a word that contains the *wo* letter string for each picture.

11. _____

12. _____

13. _____

14. _____

15. _____

16. _____

/6

Write these sentences again, replacing the bold **verb** with a more powerful one.

17. I **climbed** over the slippery rocks at the foot of the cliff.

_____

_____

18. Paul **slept** restlessly in the chair by the fire.

_____

_____

19. Maria **looked** out of the window at the view.

_____

_____

20. Peter **broke** the piggy bank to see what was inside.

_____

_____ /4

Write these words in the chart according to their **word roots**.

21–28.   telephone   octagon   prevent   impress

      pressure   megaphone   octopus   invent

phone	oct	vent	press

/8

Add the **suffix** _ish_, _ing_ or _ful_ to make **adjectives**.
You may need to alter the spellings.

29. pity   + _____ = _____

30. run   + _____ = _____

31. dare   + _____ = _____

32. style   + _____ = _____

33. beauty + _____ = _____

34. child   + _____ = _____

/6

Draw lines to match up the pairs of masculine and feminine words.

35.	cow	nephew
36.	duck	lady
37.	grandmother	bull
38.	neice	husband
39.	lord	drake
40.	wife	grandfather

/6

/40

PAPER 17

Ready, steady, shop!

High Heston is counting down to the grand opening of The Steeples this Friday.   1

The long-awaited shopping centre is home to the biggest high street names together with restaurants and bars, a bowling alley and 10-screen cinema. The centre will be the largest in the region and is bringing hundreds of new jobs to the town.

The grand opening kicks off at 9am this Friday when the Town Mayor will officially open the centre.   5
Throughout the day, shoppers will be entertained by bands and teams of jugglers, stilt-walkers and acrobats. The cinema complex is offering cut-price tickets all day Friday and several of the bars and cafes will be running special offers. On Saturday there will be puppet shows and face-painting for the children.

Centre manager Neil Barton explains: "High Heston has waited five long years for the shopping centre to open. We know that there has been some disruption to road-users during construction so we   10
wanted to put on a big show for the opening, to thank people for their patience."

The Steeples has not been without its critics. Local residents opposed the development when plans were first submitted, arguing that the roads in and around High Heston would not cope with the additional traffic the centre would bring.

Earlier in the year the centre of town was brought to a standstill when a digger preparing foundations   15
for the car park damaged gas pipes and a water main. It will take a lot to make local residents forget the three weeks of disruption they endured. Many are worried that the new car park will not be big enough for the shoppers visiting the centre from out of town, leading to more misery on the roads.

So will it all have been worth it? High Heston residents can decide for themselves, from Friday.

Circle your answers.

1. What is The Steeples?

a church   a shopping centre   a car park

2. How many screens does the cinema have?

10   5   12

3. What time does the centre open on Friday?

9.30am   9.00pm   9.00am

Answer these questions.

4–5. List two things that will entertain shoppers on opening day.

_____

_____

6. Were all the residents of High Heston excited about the shopping centre when it was first announced? Explain your answer.

_____

_____

7. What does the word *disruption* (line 10) mean?

_____

_____

8. What reason does the manager give for wanting to have an exciting launch day?

_____

_____

9. What brought the town centre to a standstill earlier in the year?

_____

_____

10. What are some people still worried about now that the centre is completed?

_____

_____

_____   /10

Find and write down one example of each
word type from this piece of writing.

Hearing voices in the kitchen, the tabby cat arched its back and sprang lightly down off the
fence. It sauntered lazily across the dewy grass towards its cat-flap.

11. noun   _____

12. pronoun   _____

13. verb   _____

14. adjective   _____

15. adverb   _____   /5

Add *it's* or *its* to complete each sentence.

16. It's funny when our puppy chases _____ tail.

17. _____ too late to take care of something when it's already broken.

18. I don't like cabbage because _____ slimy.

19. The rabbit scurried back down _____ burrow.

20. The book was muddy and _____ pages were torn.   /5

Sort these words into the table, according to whether they have the **suffix** *ible* or *able*.

21–28. edible   reliable   horrible   possible

adorable   enjoyable   responsible   valuable

ible	able

/8

Add **commas** to these sentences.

29–30. Our cat who hates water got soaked in the rain.

31. Running for the bus I tripped and fell.

32–33. On the school trip we tried canoeing abseiling climbing and raft-building.

34. After a good wash the car looked like new.

35. I needed to buy flour sugar and eggs to make the cake.

/7

Underline the **homonym** in each sentence that is used twice, each with a different meaning.

36. After we left the cinema we turned left and headed for home.

37. It isn't fair that I can't go on the big rides at the fair.

38. I saw Dad wave frantically just before the huge wave knocked me off my surfboard.

39. We sat for hours in the traffic jam, eating crisps and jam sandwiches.

40. We enjoyed reading the book so much that we couldn't wait to book tickets to see the film.

/5

/40

PAPER 18

Greg Smith,
23 Laurel Lane,
Chester
CH14 4PV

The Manager,
The Sofa Centre,
Main Street,
Chester

12th March

Dear Sir,

I am writing to complain about the sofa I bought from your store, which was delivered yesterday.

To begin with, the sofa should have been delivered last Tuesday. I took the day off work to wait for the delivery man but he did not come. I had to take another day off yesterday and then he didn't come until 6.30pm, so I could have gone to work after all.

When I unwrapped the sofa I realised that it is the wrong colour. I ordered beige but this sofa is white. We have young children so a white sofa is hardly practical. It also does not match our other furniture.

I telephoned the store this morning to complain and was told that I would have to wait three months for a replacement sofa. The manager also said that if we used the white sofa while we are waiting, we will have to pay for both sofas! What are we supposed to sit on for the next three months?

I am very disappointed by the service I have received from your company and angry that we will have to wait for a replacement sofa when the mistake was not our fault.

I would like a full refund of all the money we have paid, so that we can buy the sofa from someone else.

Yours faithfully,

Greg Smith

Circle your answers.

1. What is Mr Smith complaining about?

    a sofa   a delivery man   a shop

2. How many days did Mr Smith take off work to wait for the sofa to be delivered?

    1   2   3

3. When he unwrapped it, what was wrong with it?

it was too big   it was damaged   it was the wrong colour

4. Why is a white sofa not practical when you have young children?

_____

5. Why else does he not want a white sofa?

_____

6. How did Mr Smith find out that he would have to wait three months for the right sofa?

_____

7. Do you think it is fair that the Smith family will have to pay for both sofas if they sit on the white one while they are waiting for the replacement? Explain your answer.

_____

_____

8–9. Write down two words from the letter that describe how Mr Smith feels.

_____   _____

10. What does Mr Smith want from the sofa company?

_____

/10

Complete this **adjective** table. You may need to double the final letter of some words before adding the **suffix**.

11–18

tall big hot short

add *er*	ad *est*

/8

61

Write an interesting sentence about:

19. your school

_____

_____

20. your favourite food

_____

_____

21. a hobby you have

_____

_____

22. a place you have been on holiday

_____

_____ /4

Add the **prefix** *trans* or *tele* to each word.

23. _____atlantic

24. _____phone

25. _____vision

26. _____parent

27. _____late

28. _____scope /6

Write a word that shares the bold letter string.

29. en**ough** _____

30. l**earn** _____

31. jo**ur**ney _____

32. **sau**ce _____

33. **rice** _____

34. **fair** _____   /6

Write these sentences again, replacing
the bold word with a better **synonym**.

35. We relaxed in the **hot** sun.

_____

36. Pippa is **frightened** of the dark.

_____

37. The old house was **creepy**.

_____

38. We chose a **big** Christmas tree.

_____

39. Dad was **angry** because I was late home.

_____

40. It was **cold** last night.

_____   /6

/40

PAPER 19

Chapter 2

Very early the next morning, Mrs Bowers took us out and showed us the cowsheds, where lines of cows waited with bulging udders for milking to begin. She explained that with Mr Bowers and their two sons away fighting, she had to manage the milking herself. She was glad, she said, to have taken us in, because now she would have three extra pairs of hands.

The cows came as a shock. They were much bigger than they looked in pictures I had seen, and stronger too, as they jostled with each other. I imagined how easy it would be to be crushed between the heaving flanks of these creatures, or trampled beneath their huge hooves.

Mrs Bowers must have read my thoughts. "Don't fret about their pushing and shoving. They're eager to be free of their milk, is all. They'll be like lambs after."

She showed us how to grasp the udders and set up a rhythm to get the milk flowing. It wasn't as easy as she made it look and after five minutes of me tugging and the poor cow stamping and shuddering in impatience, there was only a thin trickle of milk in the pail like a strip of pale ribbon. I began to find, though, that the less I thought about it, the smoother my movements became and the more milk appeared in the pail. Appreciative now of my efforts, the cow settled down with great grass-scented sighs.

Calm settled over the cow shed as I milked and the dawn crept into the farmyard. The air smelt fresh and clear, untainted by smoke from burning buildings. These moments of peace experienced in the milking shed were so different, I knew, from the noisy, dangerous chaos I'd left behind, that I knew that our mother had been right to send us away.

I imagined her in London, leaving the air-raid shelter where she had spent the night, and returning to see if our little house was still standing, and to hear stories from neighbours of people who had been less fortunate.

1. Who does Mrs Bowers say does all the milking? Circle your answer.

   her husband   she does   her husband and sons

2. How many children has she taken in? Circle your answer.

   1   2   3

3. Do you think the narrator had grown up in the countryside? Give a reason for your answer.

   _____

4. Find and copy a word that describes how the cows move while they are waiting to be milked.

   _____

5. What does the narrator imagine could happen to him in the milking shed?

   _____

   _____

6. What does Mrs Bowers mean when she says that the cows will be like lambs once they have been milked?

   _____

   _____

7–8. Find and write down two phrases which describe the way things smell.

   _____

   _____

9. Why do you think the child's mother has sent them away?

   _____

   _____

10. When do you think the story is set?

   _____

   _____   /10

Add the **prefix** *auto* or *bi* to these words.

11. _____ graph

12. _____ mobile

13. _____ cycle

14. _____ focal

15. _____ biography

16. _____ lingual

17. _____ monthly

18. _____ pilot

/8

Write this sentence again, adding the capital letters and **punctuation**.

19–22. landing in egypt we couldnt believe how hot it was

_____

_____

/4

Write down a short **definition** for each word.

23. precious _____

24. eventually _____

25. consonant _____

26. brave _____

27. local _____

28. library _____

/6

Write a sentence using these **homophones**.

29. great

_____

30. grate

_____

31. waist

_____

32. waste

_____

33. weight

_____

34. wait

_____   /6

Add another word to make a **compound word**.

35. hand_____

36. rail_____

37. air_____

38. motor_____

39. wind_____

40. play_____   /6

/40

PAPER 20

In the footsteps of pharaohs

Explore the wonders of ancient Egpyt on this luxury Nile cruise-and-stay holiday.   1

The Egyptian adventure begins with seven nights aboard the five-star Nile cruise-ship Rameses III, travelling from Luxor to Aswan. Trips ashore include visits to the Valley of the Kings and Queens, Karnak and Luxor temples and a tour of the Aswan high dam. All excursions are accompanied by English and Egyptian-speaking tour guides   5
who can answer your questions about the sites visited, to ensure groups get the most from their time ashore.

Rameses III was totally refurbished earlier in the year and now offers luxurious bedroom suites with Nile views, ensuite bathrooms and separate dressing areas. The new dining facilities offer guests a choice of international cuisines prepared by award-   10
winning chefs. On deck, a plunge pool and Jacuzzis provide a chance to cool off after a morning of sightseeing on shore, with a pool-side bar providing drinks and snacks throughout the day.

Guests spend the second week of their holiday in Luxor's five-star Philae Hotel. The hotel is located in a beautiful 19th century building but offers travellers the very latest   15
in comfort. Rooms are fully air-conditioned and guests can choose from three different restaurants offering a range of hot and cold meals. The hotel has two swimming pools as well as a spa and gym. Its staff are on hand round the clock to help guests to make the most of their time in Luxor and will be happy   20
to arrange excursions to the nearby Luxor museum, the night-time sound and light shows at the temple, or a trip across the Nile to see the massive Colossi of Memnon.

Included in the price of your holiday:

• Return flights from UK to Luxor airport

• Transfers in Egypt

• Seven nights full-board aboard Rameses III

• 11 guided excursions

• Six nights half-board at Philae Hotel

• Unlimited use of pools, spa and gym at Philae Hotel

New for this season!

An optional day trip to the Abu Simbel temples, famously moved and rebuilt during the 1960s to save them from being flooded following the construction of the Aswan Dam.

1. What do you think a *cruise-and-stay holiday* (line 1) is?

_____

_____

2. What does the word *excursion* (line 5) mean?

_____

_____

3–4. Write down two of the trips guests enjoy during the cruise.

_____

_____

_____

5. Why might it be useful for tour guides to speak both English and Egyptian?

_____

6. Why is it important for guests on a Nile cruise to be able to cool off in a plunge pool or Jacuzzi?

_____

_____

7–8. List two attractions that guests staying at the Philae hotel might want to see.

_____

_____

9. Why were the Abu Simbel temples moved in the 1960s?

_____

_____

10. Do guests at the Philae Hotel have to pay extra to use the spa?

_____

_____

/10

Level 4

Complete each word with the **suffix** *al*, *ary* or *ic*.

11. station_____   **12.** person_____

13. atom_____   **14.** realist_____

15. diction_____   **16.** season_____

/6

Write down two words that share the
bold ending with each of these words.

17–18. prec**ious**   _____   _____

19–20. spec**ial**   _____   _____

21–22. c**ough**   _____   _____

/6

Write these sentences again, replacing one
of the repeated bold words with a **synonym**.

23. The storm was approaching **quickly** so we walked more **quickly** towards home.

_____

_____

24. The **funny** clown told us a **funny** joke.

_____

25. John is **unkind** to the younger children and **unkind** to his sister.

_____

_____

26. I **cut** up an onion while Dad **cut** a pepper to go in the chilli.

_____

27. Jenny was **happy** with her present and Max was **happy** with his.

_____

_____

28. The **pretty** princess had **pretty** hair.

_____

_____ /6

Write a phrase you could use to describe each thing.

29. a sunset   _____

30. a lion   _____

31. a traffic jam   _____

32. a waterfall   _____

33. a beach   _____

34. a roller coaster _____ /6

Add a suitable **adverb** to complete each sentence.

35. "Your picture is great!" said Mark, _____ .

36. The stars twinkled _____ in the inky sky.

37. The boys gobbled up the chips _____ .

38. I wrote the answers _____ on the test paper.

39. "Hello!" called the twins, _____ .

40. James built the model ship _____ /6

/40

adjectival phrase	a group of words that describe a **noun**
adjective	a word that describes a **noun**, e.g. tiny, green
adverb	a word that describes a **verb**, e.g. kindly, prettily
alphabetical order	the order of the letters in the alphabet
antonym	a word with the opposite meaning to another word, e.g tall, short
apostrophe	a **punctuation mark** used to show possession or **contraction**
collective noun	a way of describing a group of a particular thing, e.g. flock of sheep
comma	a **punctuation mark** used to indicate a pause in a sentence, or separate items in a list
common noun	a word for an ordinary thing, e.g. book, tree
compound word	a word made up of two other words, e.g. footpath
conjunction	a word used to join parts of a sentence, e.g. and, but
consonant	the letters of the alphabet that are not **vowels**
contraction	two words joined together, where an **apostrophe** marks letters that have been removed, e.g. do not = don't
definition	the meaning of a word
diminutive	a word that describes the small version of something, e.g. piglet
exclamation mark	a **punctuation mark** used at the end of sentences to show surprise or deliver an order, e.g. Stop!
full stop	a **punctuation mark** used to send most sentences
homonym	words with the same spelling but different meanings, e.g. right handed, the right answer
homophone	a word which sounds the same but has a different spelling, e.g. maid, made
noun	a word that names a thing or person
past tense	a **verb** that describes something that has already happened
personal pronoun	a **pronoun** used to replace the names of people, e.g. she, me, him
plural	more than one of something
possessive apostrophe	an apostrophe used to indicate that something belongs to someone, or something, e.g. the girl's pen

prefix	a group of letters added to the beginning of a word to alter its meaning, e.g. re, ex, co
present tense	a **verb** that describes what is happening now
pronoun	a word that can be used in the place of a **noun** e.g. he, she
proper noun	the name of a person, place, day of the week, month of the year etc, e.g. Jill, March, Rome
punctuation	marks like **full stops**, **commas** etc. used in writing to help readers understand what they are reading
question mark	a **punctuation mark** used at the end of sentences that ask a question. e.g. Is that your coat?
root word	a word that **prefixes** or **suffixes** can be added to, to make new words
singular	just one of something
speech mark	**punctuation marks** used in pairs at the start and the end of the actual words that a character says, e.g. "It's my birthday!"
suffix	a group of letters added to the end of a word to alter its meaning, e.g. less, ful, ly
syllables	the beats in a word
synonym	a word with a similar meaning to another word, e.g. large, huge
verb	a doing or being word
vowel	the letters of the alphabet a, e, i, o and u

Progress grid

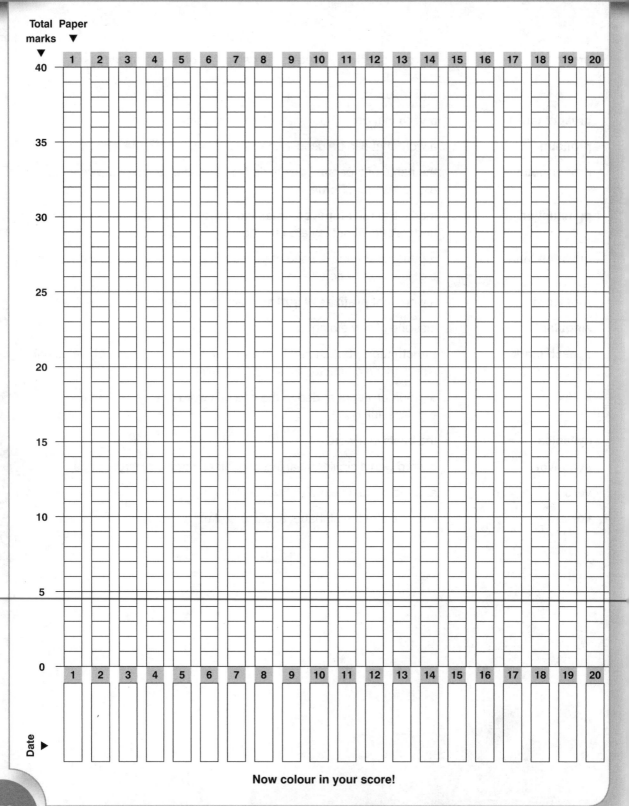

Total Paper marks ▼

Paper: 1 2 3 4 5 6 7 8 9 10 11 12 13 14 15 16 17 18 19 20

Total marks: 40 35 30 25 20 15 10 5 0

Date ▼

Now colour in your score!